W9-AJP-756

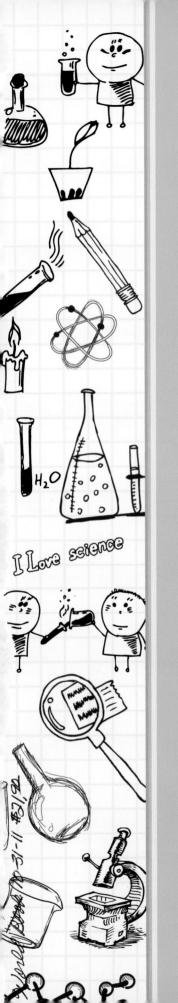

Learning Playground

Learning About Matter

WORLD BOOK

a Scott Fetzer company
Chicago
www.worldbookonline.com

World Book, Inc.
233 N. Michigan Avenue
Chicago, IL 60601
U.S.A.

For information about other World Book publications, visit our website at **http://www.worldbookonline.com** or call **1-800-WORLDBK (967-5325)**.

For information about sales to schools and libraries, call **1-800-975-3250 (United States)**; **1-800-837-5365 (Canada)**.

Library of Congress Cataloging-in-Publication Data

Learning about matter.
    p. cm. -- (Learning playground)
    Summary: "An activity-based volume that introduces early-level physical science concepts, including the properties of matter, structure of matter, states of matter, physical and chemical changes to matter, compounds and elements, and the periodic table. Features include a glossary, an additional resource list, and an index"-- Provided by publisher.
    Includes index.
    ISBN 978-0-7166-0234-7
    1. Matter--Constitution--Juvenile literature. 2. Matter-- Properties--Juvenile literature. I. World Book, Inc.
    QC173.16.L43 2012
    530--dc22
                        2011011522

STAFF
Executive Committee
President: Donald D. Keller
Vice President and
    Editor in Chief: Paul A. Kobasa
Vice President, Marketing/
    Digital Products: Sean Klunder
Vice President, International: Richard Flower
Director, Human Resources: Bev Ecker

Editorial
Associate Manager, Supplementary
    Publications: Cassie Mayer
Editor: Mike DuRoss
Researcher: Annie Brodsky
Manager, Contracts & Compliance
    (Rights & Permissions): Loranne K. Shields
Indexer: David Pofelski

Graphics and Design
Manager: Tom Evans
Coordinator, Design Development and
    Production: Brenda B. Tropinski
Associate Designer: Matt Carrington
Photographs Editor: Kathy Creech

Pre-Press and Manufacturing
Director: Carma Fazio
Manufacturing Manager: Barbara Podczerwinski
Production/Technology Manager:
    Anne Fritzinger

Learning Playground
Set ISBN: 978-0-7166-0225-5

Printed in Malaysia by TWP Sdn Bhd, Johor Bahru
1st printing July 2011

Acknowledgments:
The publishers gratefully acknowledge the following sources for photography. All illustrations were prepared by WORLD BOOK unless otherwise noted.

Cover: Dreamstime; iStockphoto; WORLD BOOK photo; Shutterstock

David Pearson, Alamy Images 51; Dreamstime 4, 5, 7, 12, 28, 31, 35, 36, 38, 40, 42, 57, 59; istockphoto 22, 34; Shutterstock 4, 5, 6, 7, 8, 12, 13, 14, 15, 16, 17, 18, 19, 21, 23, 24, 25, 28, 29, 39, 43, 50, 54, 56, 57, 58, 59; Tom Tropinski 37, 48-49.

Table of Contents

There is a glossary on page 62. Terms defined in the glossary are in type that **looks like this** on their first appearance on any spread (two facing pages).

What Is Matter?

Matter is all around you. What kinds of matter do you see in your backyard?

Everything is made of matter. Matter is anything that takes up space. A rock, a dandelion, a rabbit, and a puddle of water are all matter. And you are matter, too! There is matter in everything around you.

Matter takes many different forms. All nonliving things, such as rocks and water, are made of matter.

Rabbits and all other living things are made of matter.

Air is invisible, but it is made of matter. We can see the effects of moving air as wind.

Even air is matter. You don't feel how much air weighs because most things are heavier than air. But air has weight. And it takes up space. You feel it take up space when you breathe. You see it take up space when you blow up a balloon.

Measuring Matter

We can measure matter in several ways. For example, we can measure an object's **mass.**

Mass is the amount of matter in an object. Mass is like weight. Heavy objects have a lot of mass. Light objects have little mass.

We can also measure an object's **volume.** Volume measures the amount of space something takes up. An object's volume is a measure of its size.

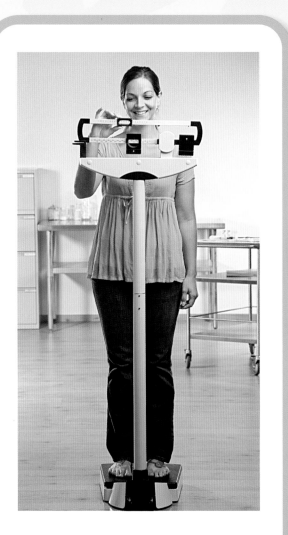

Mass

To weigh something means to find out its mass, or how much matter it has. When you weigh yourself, you are finding out the amount of matter that makes up your body.

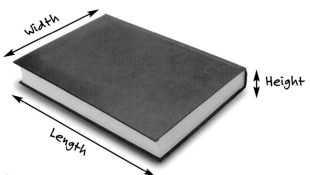

Volume

Both solids and liquids have volume. The volume of a rectangle-shaped solid can be found by multiplying its **dimensions**—length × width × height. The volume of a liquid is often measured in special containers that have marks showing different volumes.

Mass and volume may seem like the same thing, but they're quite different. For example, a bowling ball and a balloon may have similar volume. But the bowling ball is much heavier. It is more dense. In other words, it has more mass in the same amount of space. **Density** is the amount of mass in a given volume.

Density

A bowling ball and a balloon are about the same size. But the bowling ball is much denser. It has more matter in the same amount of space.

HOW MUCH DOES IT WEIGH?

In everyday use, weight and **mass** can mean the same thing. For example, your weight is the amount of matter that makes up your body. In science, weight is the measure of the pull of gravity on an object.

The activities on these pages use weight to determine and compare the mass of different objects. How well can you estimate the weight of things? Try these activities to find out!

MATERIALS

- Bathroom scale
- 5 grocery bags
- Assortment of heavy objects, such as books or rocks
- Pencil
- Paper

DIRECTIONS

Use a Bathroom Scale

1. Put several objects in each grocery bag. Lift the bags to see how heavy they feel.

2. Number the bags in order, from the one you think is heaviest to the one you think is lightest.

3. Weigh each bag on the scale. Did you put the bags in the correct order?

4. Draw a bar graph to show the weight of each bag.

Use a Balance Scale

1. Punch a hole in the flap of each envelope. Thread string through the holes and tie one envelope to each end of the hanger.

2. Hang the hanger on the clothesline. Adjust the envelopes so the hanger hangs evenly. Tape the strings to the hanger.

3. Pick up two different objects. Try to guess which one is heavier. Test your guess by putting one object in each envelope. The hanger will tip toward the heavier object.

4. Try several pairs of objects. The more you practice, the better you'll get at estimating which object is heavier!

MATERIALS

- 2 manila envelopes
- Hole punch
- String
- Scissors
- Hanger
- Clothesline
- Tape
- Small objects to weigh, such as crayons, checkers, and feathers

HOW MUCH WILL IT HOLD?

Do you like to cook? Measurement is an important part of cooking. Most recipes call for specific amounts of each ingredient, such as 2 cups of flour or 1 teaspoon of lemon juice.

Cups and teaspoons are two units for measuring **volume.** The volume of a container is the amount it can hold. You can measure volume without special measuring cups or measuring spoons.

MATERIALS

- Pitcher of water
- Large pan of uncooked rice or dried beans
- Several sizes of plastic drinking cups, bowls, and other containers
- Small scoop

DIRECTIONS

1. Choose a drinking cup and a bowl. Estimate how many of those cups full of water will fit in the bowl.

2. Fill the drinking cup with water and pour it into the bowl. Continue until the bowl is full. How many of these drinking cups of water does it take to fill the bowl? How close was your estimate?

3. Repeat steps 1 and 2 with other sizes of drinking cups and bowls.

4. Choose two different-shaped containers. Which one do you think has the larger volume?

5. Use the scoop to fill both containers with rice or beans. Count the number of scoops you put in each container. Which container holds more? Was your estimate correct?

6. Repeat steps 4 and 5 with other pairs of containers.

Units of Measurement

In addition to measuring **mass** and **volume,** we can also measure an object's length and other **dimensions.**

Numbers are an important part of measuring, but they're not the only part. When someone asks how tall you are, you don't say "52" or "132." If you're in the United States, you say, "52 inches." If you're in England, you say, "132 centimeters." Inches and centimeters are units of measurement.

People can measure the size of objects using a tape measure or other measuring tool.

Inches are part of the inch-pound system of measurement commonly used in the United States. One inch is as long as this blue box:

Other units of length in the inch-pound system are called feet, yards, and miles. There are 12 inches in 1 foot. There are 3 feet in 1 yard. A mile is much longer. There are 5,280 feet in 1 mile.

In the late 1700's, the French government asked scientists to invent a new system of weights and measures. The scientists wanted the system to be simple and based on facts in science. That's how the metric system was created. It is used in most countries of the world.

Centimeters are part of the metric system. One centimeter is the length of this orange box: ⟶

Other units of length in the metric system are meters and kilometers.

The metric system is based on 10's. For example, here are units of length in the metric system:

10 millimeters = 1 centimeter
10 centimeters = 1 decimeter
10 decimeters = 1 meter
1,000 meters = 1 kilometer

Architects use measurements when designing buildings.

HOW LONG IS IT?

How long is your foot? How about your hand? You can measure the length of your own hand and foot as well as many objects around your home.

MATERIALS

- Paper clips
- Playing cards
- Paper
- Pencil
- Spoon
- Toothbrush
- Marker
- Fork
- Crayon
- Magazine
- Baseball bat

DIRECTIONS

1. Make a row of paper clips to measure each of the objects that follow. Don't leave any space between the paper clips. Record your measurements on the paper.

   a. a pencil

   b. a toothbrush

   c. a spoon

8 paper clips   7 paper clips   4 paper clips

2. Estimate the lengths of the following objects in paper clips. Then measure them. Write the estimated lengths and actual lengths on a piece of paper. How close were your estimates?

   a. a marker

   b. a fork

   c. a crayon

   d. your hand, from wrist to fingertip

   e. your foot, from heel to tip of the longest toe

3. Use playing cards to measure the lengths of the following objects. Record your measurements on the paper. You could also make a bar graph to show the lengths.

   a. a magazine

   b. a baseball bat

   c. your bed

Properties of Matter

Things that describe matter are called **properties.** Anything we can describe with our senses is a property. For example, the flavor of food is a property. The feel of a soft blanket is a property. Color, shape, feel, taste, and smell are all properties we observe with our senses.

There are several properties of matter we cannot find out with just our senses. Can you tell if something can float just by looking at it? If you saw a magnet sitting on a table by itself, would you know that it attracts metals?

Shiny objects reflect light, creating a mirror image.

The ability to float and magnetism (the force that attracts certain kinds of metals) are invisible properties of matter. The ability to conduct (move) heat and electricity are properties, too. **Mass, volume,** and **density** are properties that we can measure.

← This dog's fur feels soft to the touch.

Rough surfaces are often dull in color.
↓

Floating and Sinking

Have you ever noticed how the water in the bathtub rises when you get in? This happens because your body weight pushes the water aside, or displaces it.

What happens when you get into a larger body of water? You float! Your body pushes aside enough water to equal your weight. But the water also pushes back against your body, so you float. This is called buoyancy (BOY uhn see). Buoyancy is the upward push of displaced water.

A beach ball has a lot of buoyancy. It easily floats on top of water.

Try this!

See how the shape of an object affects whether it will float or sink. Roll a chunk of clay into a ball and put it into a bowl of water. It sinks. Flatten the clay and put it into the water. It sinks. Flatten the clay more and curve the edges up, like a small bowl. Put it into the water. Does it float? If the sides are high enough, it should. Try dividing the clay in half and making two small bowls. Put one bowl on top of the other. Pinch the edges so you have a hollow ball. Does this shape float? How are these shapes like a boat?

If you could weigh the water your body displaced, it would be equal to the pressure of the water pushing up on your body. The pressure pushing up cancels out your weight pushing down.

So why do some objects sink? Objects that are heavier than the same amount of water sink in water. When you throw a rock into the water, it weighs more than the amount of water it displaces, so it sinks.

This ship weighs 50,000 tons (50,800 metric tons).

The ship floats in the water, despite its weight.

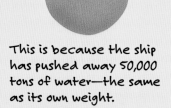

This is because the ship has pushed away 50,000 tons of water—the same as its own weight.

Large, heavy cargo ships float because they displace the same amount of water as their weight.

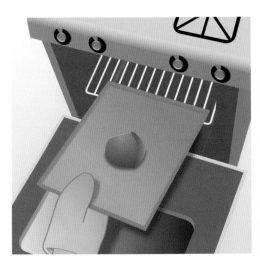
MATERIALS

- 20 or more samples of different materials (wood, salt, a rock, a leaf, aluminum foil)
- Baking tray
- Oven
- Piece of cloth
- Hammer
- Bowl
- Water
- Pen or pencil
- Paper

Try this experiment to test the **properties** of different kinds of matter. You'll need to collect about 20 or more materials from in and around your home. It is best to start with simple materials like a piece of wood, a spoonful of salt, or a rock. Try not to collect things that are made up of more than one material.

The data sheet on the next page will help you to organize your collection and to discover the properties of each material. Some materials have already been written down and described on the sheet to show you how. Draw up your own data sheet using these ideas as a starting point. With practice, you can invent your own tests to suit the types of materials in your collection. If you do invent your own test, always check with an adult first to make sure it is safe to do.

Ask a teacher or other adult to help you with this experiment.

DIRECTIONS

1. Place a small sample on a baking tray and place it in a cold oven. Heat up the oven, then switch it off and wait until it is cool before removing the sample. **Do this with adult supervision.**

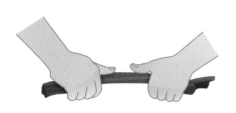

2. Try bending a larger sample with your hands.

3. Wrap each sample in a cloth and hit it with a hammer. **Do this with adult supervision.** Does the sample shatter?

4. Leave each sample in a bowl of water. Does it float or sink? Does it change if you leave it there for a few days?

5. When you have tested your materials, fill in the results on your data sheet. Your list of results will be the different properties of the materials.

	Material	Heating not burning	Bending	Hammering	Adding water	Natural, artificial, or both
1.	wood	burns	splinters	dents	floats	natural
2.	salt	nothing	—	powders	dissolves	natural
3.	rock					
4.	leaf					
5.	twig					
6.	aluminum foil					
7.						
8.						

What Is Matter Made Of?

What is in a sand castle? Millions and millions of tiny grains of sand. The many grains of sand are packed together to make a single shape, like a castle with towers, walls, and bridges.

A single grain of sand is made of many tiny atoms.

And what are you made of? Millions and millions of tiny bits, each one even smaller than a grain of sand. You and everything around you—people and animals, cars, rocks, water, and even the air—are made of tiny bits that are put together in different ways.

These bits of matter are called **atoms** (AT uhmz). Atoms are much smaller than a grain of sand. In fact, they are so small that you can't see individual atoms. But if you could see them, you would find that atoms are made up of even smaller pieces.

Atoms are made of even smaller particles called protons, neutrons, and electrons. Protons and neutrons are at the center of the atom. Electrons circle around the protons and neutrons.

Nucleus ——

Proton
Neutron
Electron

Even though atoms are so small that you can't see them, they still have weight, and they take up space.

Atoms can bond (become connected) to one another. When two or more atoms bond together, they become a **molecule** (MAHL uh kyool).

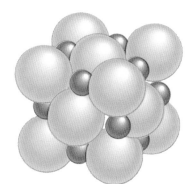

Sodium

Chlorine

Chemical bonds between sodium and chlorine atoms lock them together. They then form a molecule called sodium chloride.

The air, water, trees, and other natural things are made of atoms. Bridges and other human-made objects are made of atoms, too.

Elements and Compounds

How many kinds of matter are there? So many that if you started to count them, you probably would never finish!

Sulfur

Copper

But if you could sort out the **atoms** in all that matter, you would find that there are just over 100 kinds. The type of atom depends on how many protons it has. Protons are positively charged particles that are part of the nucleus (center) of an atom.

Some kinds of matter are made up of only one kind of atom. These kinds of matter are called chemical **elements** (EHL uh muhnts).

Gold is an element. A piece of pure gold is made of just gold atoms. Iron is an element, too. It is made of just iron atoms.

Gold

But most kinds of matter are made of two or more different kinds of atoms joined together in a **molecule.** These kinds of matter are called **compounds** (KAHM powndz).

Water is a compound made of the element oxygen (AHK suh juhn) and the element hydrogen (HY druh juhn). By themselves, oxygen and hydrogen are invisible gases. You cannot see them. But when they join together, they make a liquid you can see—water.

Hydrogen atoms

Oxygen atom

Water molecule

Each molecule of water is made of two hydrogen atoms and one oxygen atom.

← Salt is a compound of the elements sodium and chlorine.

MODEL CHEMICAL COMPOUNDS

Make your own models of chemical **compounds** using the examples on these pages.

MATERIALS

- Different-colored modeling clay
- Drinking straws
- Ruler
- Marker
- Scissors

DIRECTIONS

1. Roll out balls in different colors of the modeling clay to represent the different **elements.** Carbon should be the largest ball and hydrogen should be the smallest. Nitrogen and oxygen should be medium size. The list below shows you how many balls you need to make.

Carbon	Red	4
Hydrogen	Yellow	13
Nitrogen	Green	1
Oxygen	Blue	3

2. Using the ruler, mark off 1-inch (2.54-centimeter) sections on the drinking straws. You will need a total of 21 sections to make the four models in this activity.

3. Follow the pictures to create models of some common chemical compounds. For example, the compound ammonia has one nitrogen **atom** and three hydrogen atoms arranged like this:

Ammonia

Now make models for these compounds:

4. Methane is made of one carbon atom and four hydrogen atoms. It is used in gas stoves for cooking.

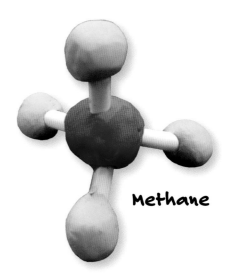

Methane

5. Carbon dioxide is the gas you breathe out. It is also created by the burning of any substance that contains carbon, such as coal, gasoline, and wood. Plants use carbon dioxide to make food. Carbon dioxide is made of one carbon atom and two oxygen atoms.

Carbon dioxide

6. Ethanol can be used as a fuel to power vehicles. It is made of two carbon atoms, six hydrogen atoms, and one oxygen atom.

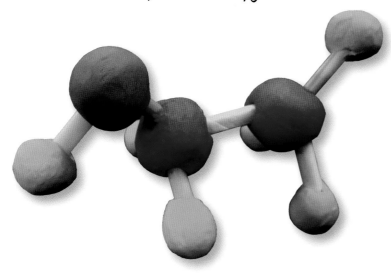

Ethanol/ethyl alcohol

There are many different chemicals that you can make models of. Ask your teacher or librarian to help you look up pictures of other chemical compounds. For example, you could build the compounds for baking soda (sodium bicarbonate), water, and propane.

What Are States of Matter?

Solids have size and shape and can be broken apart.

A stone wall is hard, water is wet, and the air is invisible. But they are all matter, and they are all made up of **molecules.** Even so, they behave in different ways. So we say that they are different states of matter. Solids, liquids, and gases are the three basic states of matter.

Stone is a solid. It has a shape of its own. The molecules in most solids are very close together. They are stuck in one position, helping them to keep their shape.

Water is a liquid. It has no shape of its own. It takes the shape of the container it is in. Molecules in most liquids are farther apart than molecules in a solid, but they still touch one another. They are not stuck in one position. They can slide around and take any shape.

Liquids move freely and have no shape of their own.

Wind is made of invisible gases.

Air is a gas. It has no shape of its own, either. Its molecules are far apart and hardly touch one another. Molecules of a gas bounce around so easily that they can squeeze into a small balloon or spread out to fill a big room.

The molecules in ice do not move around much. They cling together to form a solid.

The molecules in liquid water move around freely.

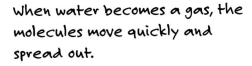

When water becomes a gas, the molecules move quickly and spread out.

MEALTIME MATTER

Like everything else in the world, the foods and drinks we enjoy are made of matter. They can be in the form of solids, liquids, or gases. Many foods change from one form to another when we change their temperature. Using a separate piece of paper and a pencil, match the foods and drinks listed in the boxes with the numbered clues. Answers appear at the bottom of page 31.

FOODS

a. Buttered toast
b. Soda
c. Soft-boiled egg
d. Spaghetti
e. Soup
f. Ice cream
g. Fried fish
h. Frozen orange juice
i. Salad

Breakfast

1. I start out as a cold solid. After you stir me with a clear liquid, you can drink me.

2. I start out as a soft, flat solid. When you heat me, I turn crisp. I taste good when I'm spread with a yellow solid that melts.

3. I start out as a white solid filled with soft, gooey liquid. If you boil me for three minutes, part of me turns into a solid. You can draw a face on me before you crack me and eat me.

Lunch

4. I'm a cold liquid filled with tiny bubbles of gas.

5. I'm a liquid mixed with chunks of solids. You can eat me with a spoon or slurp me from a mug.

6. I'm chunks of solids dipped in thick liquid. Then I'm cooked in a hot liquid until I'm crispy and golden.

Dinner

7. I start out as thin, hard sticks. When you boil me in a liquid, I get soft. I taste delicious with a warm, red liquid poured over me.

8. I'm all different kinds of crunchy raw solids. You can toss me in a bowl with a bit of oily or creamy liquid.

9. I'm a sweet, frozen solid that you scoop out of a container. If I get warm, I melt into a liquid.

ANSWERS:
1. h   6. g
2. a   7. d
3. c   8. i
4. b   9. f
5. e

Heating Matter

When matter is heated or cooled, it can change states. For example, if you heat ice cubes in a pan, the ice will melt into water. And after a while, the water will boil and turn into **water vapor**—a gas. What makes the ice cubes change?

Ice melts because something happens to its **molecules.** Heat energy makes the molecules move faster. As the molecules speed up, they begin to slide past one another. Then the ice changes from a solid to a liquid—water.

Heat changes ice cubes from a solid to a liquid and then to a gas.

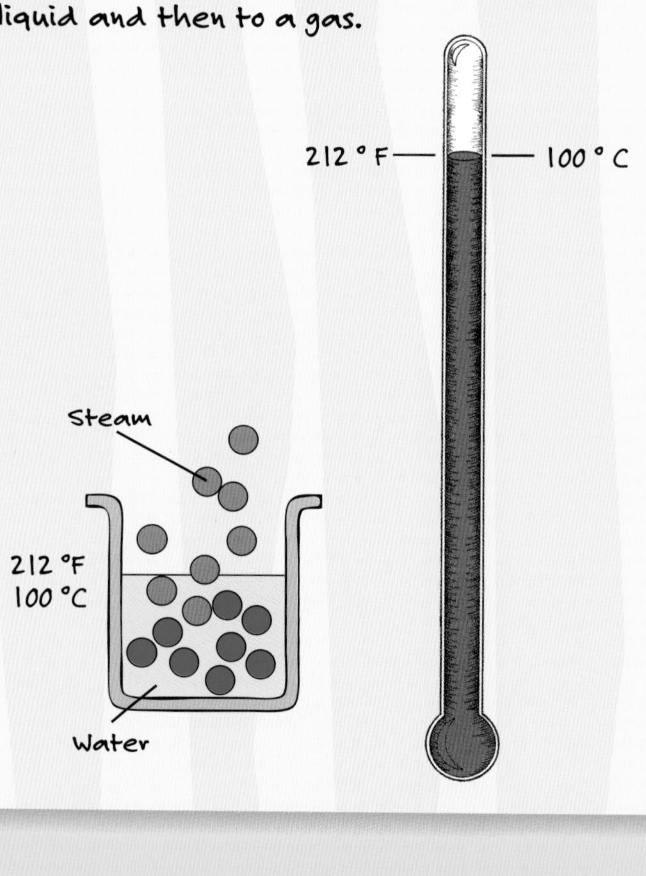

212 °F —— 100 °C

Steam

212 °F
100 °C

Water

The boiling point is the temperature at which a liquid turns into a gas.

Heat speeds up the molecules in liquids, too. So as the molecules speed up, they move farther apart. They move too fast to stick together. Eventually, the liquid **evaporates** (ih VAP uh rayts). It becomes a gas. The molecules in a gas move so fast that they fly apart.

And that's what happens when water boils. Heat makes the molecules roll and tumble faster and faster in the pan. When the water molecules are moving fast enough, they become a gas. You can tell that water vapor has formed when you see a cloud of steam rising from the boiling water.

When matter changes states, it undergoes a physical change. The matter may look different, but its **properties** are still the same. It's still made of the same materials.

How Heat Changes Molecules

Cold molecules stay close together.

Heat makes the molecules speed up and move away from one another.

As molecules speed up, they lose their pull on one another.

Cooling Matter

Sometimes in cool weather, the insides of windows look cloudy. They are covered with a thin film of water. Where does this water come from?

It comes from **water vapor**—water **molecules** mixed with the air inside the house. The water collects on the windows when the glass is cool.

Water vapor is a gas. The molecules of water vapor are as warm as the air around them in the house, so they move very fast. But when the molecules hit the cool glass in the window, they lose heat. As the molecules grow cooler, they move closer together and slow down. When they are moving slowly enough, they **condense** (kuhn DEHNS), or bundle together. They turn into tiny drops of liquid.

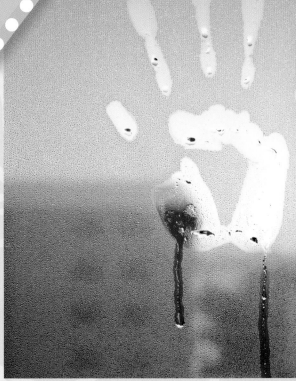

Condensation occurs when warm air hits a cool surface, such as a glass window.

Cooling Water Molecules

At room temperature, water molecules move about freely.

As water gets colder, the molecules move closer together.

When water freezes, the molecules move apart and form stiff crystals. The water becomes ice.

Sometimes when the weather is very cold, the glass in the windows gets much colder than the air inside the house. Then the molecules of water vapor lose even more heat when they touch the glass. They slow down much more and move closer together. When they get close enough to pull hard on one another, they freeze. Then the window is covered with frost—thin, feathery bits of solid ice.

On really cold days, condensation can cause frost to form on the inside of a window.

Try this!

See how temperature affects the molecules in a gas by trying this experiment. Blow up a sausage-shaped balloon and tie the end. Tie a piece of thread around the balloon, just tightly enough so that the thread doesn't move. Put the balloon in a refrigerator or freezer overnight or longer. Take out the balloon. Feel how the balloon is different. As the air warms up, the balloon changes. Can you explain what has happened to the gas inside the balloon?

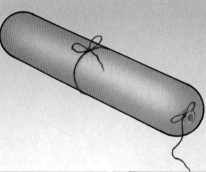

MOVING MOLECULES

Try this experiment to see how temperataure affects the motion of **molecules**.

MATERIALS

- 2 large glasses
- Blue and red food coloring
- Boiling water
- Iced water

I Love science

DIRECTIONS

1. Fill one glass with cold water. Add ice cubes and let it stand for a few minutes to make the water really cold. Remove the ice cubes. Wait until the water is still. Then add one drop of blue food coloring to the water. Watch how the color moves through the water.

2. Ask an adult to help you fill the other glass with boiling water. Wait until the water is still. Then place one drop of red food coloring in the glass. How does the color move in this glass? How does it compare to the cold water?

Cold Water

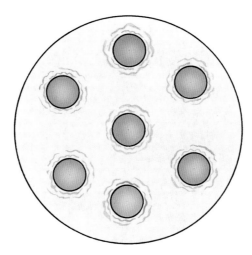

How fast does the food coloring spread in each glass? The molecules of hot water are moving faster than the molecules of cold water. This causes the food coloring to spread much faster in the glass of hot water.

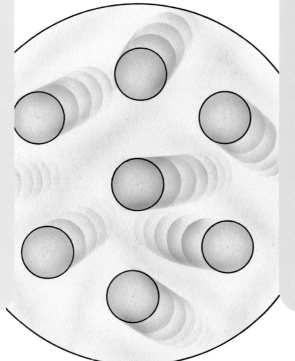

Hot Water

As Warm as Toast

Cold butter on hot toast doesn't stay cold for very long. Some of the heat from the toast passes into the butter, and so the butter becomes warm, too. The heat is a form of energy.

Heat energy can spread. Heat energy always flows from something warmer to something cooler. The movement of **molecules** passes the heat along.

A slice of toast is a solid piece of bread. But the molecules in the bread move. They wriggle and jiggle, even though they are held together. As the bread is toasted, the heat from the toaster makes the molecules speed up.

When you spread cold butter onto hot toast, some of the fast-moving toast molecules (red) bump into the slow-moving butter molecules (blue).

Cold butter is solid, too. But its molecules move very slowly. When you spread the cold butter onto the hot toast, some of the fast-moving toast molecules bump into the slow-moving butter molecules. That makes the butter molecules move faster. The jiggling motion moves from molecule to molecule until the butter is soft and warm. If the butter gets warm enough, it becomes a liquid.

Try this!

Put five coins with different dates in a small box. Show them to some friends and explain that you will read your friends' minds. While your back is turned, have your friends choose one of the coins and remember its date. Ask each friend to hold the coin tightly in one hand for a moment and to concentrate on the date. When everyone has had a turn, have the last person drop the coin in the box. Turn around right away and touch each coin lightly. Four of the coins will be cool—but the fifth will be warm because it has taken heat energy from your friends' hands. Pick that coin, read the date, and amaze your friends!

What Makes a Hot-Air Balloon Fly?

A balloon filled with hot air can lift people up in the air.

Did you know that some people fly using a bag of hot air? Of course, the "bag" is a huge hot-air balloon.

When air is heated, its **molecules** speed up and begin to push on one another. This makes the air expand. The molecules of hot air push farther and farther apart until only a few molecules take up a great deal of space.

The molecules of hot air that fill a balloon are farther apart than the molecules of colder air outside the balloon. So the hot air weighs much less than the colder air. Because the hot air is lighter, it rises. It pushes up inside the balloon. When the push is strong enough, it lifts the balloon high into the sky.

GROWING GAS

See for yourself how heated gas expands to fill a balloon. Ask a teacher or adult to help you with this experiment. **Never use the stove without an adult's permission.**

MATERIALS

- Pot or saucepan
- Water
- Small glass bottle
- Stove
- Balloon
- Paper
- Pen or pencil

DIRECTIONS

1. Fill the pot or saucepan with enough water to cover most of the glass bottle. Fill the glass bottle with enough water so that it stands upright in the pot. Stretch the mouth of the balloon over the mouth of the bottle.

2. Place the pot of water on the burner. Make sure the bottle is at least 2 inches (5 centimeters) from the side of the pot.

3. Think about what will happen to the water, the air inside the bottle, and the balloon when heat is applied. Write down your prediction.

4. Ask an adult to turn on the burner and watch as the water comes to a boil. Did your prediction come true? Why or why not? Record your results. (Make sure you turn off the burner before the water boils away.)

What Makes a Pot Lid Bounce?

You don't have to watch a covered cooking pot to know when the food or water inside it is boiling. The lid will begin to bounce up and down when the water boils. The push that moves the lid comes from **water vapor**.

When water boils, the water vapor escapes from the pot as steam.

As the water inside the pot is heated, its **molecules** take up energy. That energy makes the molecules speed up and push hard against one another. When the water is hot enough, some of it changes from a liquid into a gas.

Heat causes water molecules to speed up. When they get hot enough, they change into a gas.

The molecules of gases move around more and are farther apart than the molecules of liquids. So the water expands into a gas. It takes up much more space than the hot liquid water did. But there is only one place where the water vapor can escape—through the spaces around the pot lid. It squeezes out with a hard push, and the push bounces the lid up and down. Steam starts to push out from the sides of the lid, too.

Steam is made of very tiny droplets of liquid water. Steam can be used to push the moving parts of machines. The machines run ships, trains, and factories that make electricity. Such big machines need very strong pushes from expanding gas, so huge amounts of water must be boiled.

The heat energy in steam is converted into electricity at power plants.

The first locomotives were powered by steam engines.

Activity > MAKING CHANGES

All around us, there are solids, liquids, and gases. So in everything around us, **molecules** behave in certain ways. They hang together tightly, slide around one another, or move about freely in space. By heating or cooling matter, it's easy to change matter from one state to another. The activities on pages 44–46 and the observations that follow will show you how!

DIRECTIONS

Activity 1

1. Make sure the glasses are the same temperature as the room. Put an ice cube in the first glass, a small piece of butter in the second glass, and a coin in the third glass.

2. Now leave the glasses for 10 to 20 minutes. Which of the three materials has melted?

MATERIALS

- 3 glasses of the same size
- 2 ice cubes
- Cold butter
- 1 coin
- Metal pan
- Water
- Metal jar lid big enough to fit over the glasses. (If there is cardboard in the lid, remove it.)

Activity 2

Have an adult help you pour 1 inch (2.5 centimeters) of hot water from the tap into the pan. Set the glasses from Activity 1 in the pan and leave them for 10 minutes. What changes do you see in the materials in the glasses?

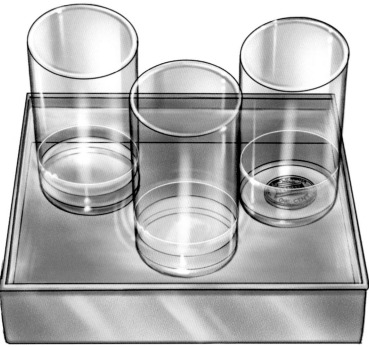

MAKING CHANGES

Activity 3

Have an adult help you fill one glass half full with hot water from the tap. Set the jar lid on the glass, upside down. Then place an ice cube on the lid. After five minutes, remove the ice cube and carefully remove the lid. What do you see on the side of the lid that covered the glass?

OBSERVATIONS:

Activity 1

At room temperature, some of the ice cube melts. The butter doesn't melt, but it gets softer. The coin doesn't change.

Activity 2

The hot water makes the **molecules** speed up. Much more of the ice cube melts. The butter melts, too. But the **atoms** in the coin don't speed up much, so the coin doesn't melt.

Activity 3

There are drops of water on the lid. Some molecules in the hot water changed into gas. But when they hit the cold lid, they slowed down, **condensed,** and became a liquid again.

Sand mixed with water is a kind of suspension. Eventually, the mixture separates.

Mixing Matter

Try this experiment: Fill two glasses with water. Then take a spoonful of sand and mix it into one glass. Now pour a spoonful of salt into the second glass. Stir the water for about a minute.

What happened when you mixed the two different substances with water? The sand probably settled to the bottom once the water stopped moving. If you stirred the salt water long enough, the salt probably seemed to have disappeared.

The salt water and sand water are two different kinds of **mixtures.** A mixture is a physical combination of substances.

In the sand and water mixture, the two substances remained separate. This kind of mixture is called a **suspension.**

In a suspension, particles of one substance float in another substance. But the particles are more dense than the substance they float in, so they settle to the bottom over time if left alone. And they can be filtered (separated) fairly easily from the substance they are floating in.

In the second mixture, the salt particles dissolved in the water. This means they broke up into super-tiny pieces and spread out evenly in the water. This kind of mixture is called a **solution.** The substances in a solution are very thoroughly and evenly mixed.

Salt and water is a kind of solution. The two substances blend together evenly.

If you stir table salt into a glass of water, the salt will dissolve. The water is a solvent (liquid), and the salt is a solute. The resulting salty water is a solution. In a salt solution, the **atoms** of sodium and chlorine are surrounded by **molecules** of water.

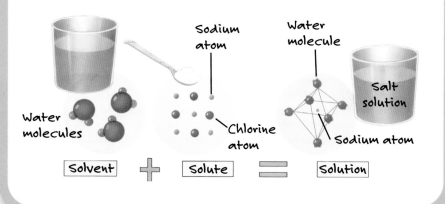

Water molecules

Sodium atom

Chlorine atom

Water molecule

Salt solution

Sodium atom

Solvent ✚ Solute ═ Solution

Separating Parts of a Mixture

Sometimes we need to separate **mixtures.** Some mixtures are easy to separate. For example, if you had a box of red and blue pens, you could easily separate them into two groups. Some sand is a mixture of solid particles of iron and the mineral quartz. Separating iron from the sand is fairly easy. Just drag a magnet through the sand. The iron should stick to the magnet.

Simple mixtures, such as a group of buttons of different colors, can be easily separated.

It is often more difficult to separate a **solution.** How can we remove the salt from salt water? The salt is mixed thoroughly but it doesn't bond to the water, so it can be separated, but how? We can wait for the water to **evaporate** (turn into a gas). The salt will not evaporate. The evaporation leaves behind a white crust of salt. We could also boil the water. Water evaporates more quickly when it is boiling.

People separate the salt from salt water in large shallow pools. Eventually, the sun causes the water to evaporate, leaving the salt behind.

MIXING THINGS UP

Which substances make a **solution** with water, and which ones make a **suspension?** How can you tell the difference between a solution and a suspension? Try this activity to find out!

MATERIALS

- 4 large jars, all the same size, and 4 drinking glasses
- Warm water
- 4 spoons, all the same size
- Small can (6 fl. oz) of pulp-free orange juice concentrate
- Flour
- Salt
- Food coloring
- 4 coffee filters, all the same kind
- 4 rubber bands
- Flashlight

DIRECTIONS

1. Fill the jars halfway with water. Put a spoonful of salt into jar #1 and stir thoroughly. Stir a spoonful of flour into jar #2. Stir several spoonfuls of the orange juice concentrate into jar #3. Squeeze a few drops of the food coloring into jar #4. Be sure to use the same amount and temperature of water in each jar. Stir the **mixtures** equally.

2. Shine the flashlight into each jar. Which jars can you clearly see through? In which ones can you see particles?

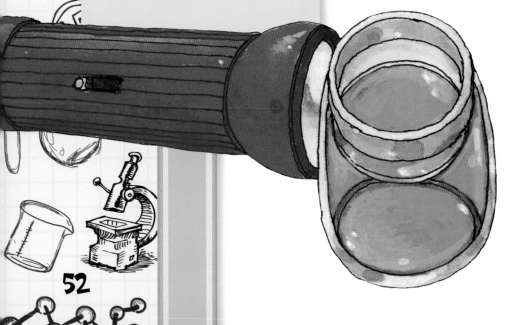

3. Pair an empty glass with each jar. Put a filter on each glass. Use a rubber band to hold the filter in place.

4. Carefully pour one-third of the mixture in each jar through the filter into its paired glass. What happens in each glass?

5. Leave the jars with their remaining mixtures undisturbed overnight. What do you see in each jar the next day?

6. Write or draw what you see in each jar. Which jar held a solution? A suspension? How do you know? What other items can you test?

Try the experiment again. Set up another jar and glass and use plain water. Try mixing other materials with water, such as sand, cornstarch, or sugar. Replace the water with vinegar or oil.

What Are Chemical Changes?

When certain substances mix, they transform into new substances. They undergo a chemical change.

A chemical change is a change in **molecules.** When a chemical change occurs, the **atoms** in the molecules form new patterns. Sometimes atoms from two kinds of molecules rearrange themselves as three or more new kinds of molecules. In other cases, they join as one molecule. Each new substance may have a different color, taste, or feel. It may behave differently.

Rust is a kind of chemical change. It forms when iron undergoes a chemical reaction with oxygen in the air.

Often heat must be applied to start the atoms moving out of their original patterns. Other times the motion of the atoms produces heat.

The forming, rearranging, or breaking apart of molecules is called a chemical reaction. Every chemical change involves at least one chemical reaction.

Burning is a sign of a chemical change. The wood reacts with oxygen in the air to make ash, smoke, and other substances.

Activity

RUSTING

In this experiment, decide whether a chemical change is involved. Record your observations and check them against the observations in the upside-down box on this page.

MATERIALS

- 4 glass jars
- Permanent marker
- Water
- 4 iron nails
- Stove
- Cooking oil
- Salt

DIRECTIONS

1. Fill the first jar with enough room-temperature water to cover the bottom. Put a nail in the water. The top should stick up above the water's surface. Mark this jar "1" with the marker.

2. Put a nail in the second jar with no water. Mark this jar "2."

3. Ask an adult to help you boil some water to remove any oxygen that may be mixed with the water. Put enough of this water in the third jar to cover the nail completely. Pour a little oil on top to keep air out of the water. Mark this jar "3."

4. Fill the fourth jar with enough room-temperature water to cover the bottom. Before you put the nail in, stir plenty of salt into the water to make a strong salt **solution.** Mark this jar "4."

AFTER A FEW DAYS:

Jar 1:
The nail will rust because there is air and water in the jar.

Jar 2:
The nail will not rust very much because there is no water.

Jar 3:
The nail will not rust very much even though it is in water. This is because the oil keeps out the air.

Jar 4:
The nail will rust because there is water and air. The salt in the water speeds up the rusting, so the nail will rust more quickly.

Love science

H₂O

55

Grouping Matter

Every day you use many different kinds of matter. You probably use a metal knife and fork when you eat. You write on paper, which is made from wood. And you breathe in oxygen, a gas. You know that these kinds of matter are different from one another, but how?

Copper is a good conductor of electricity. Copper wire carries electric current inside homes, factories, and offices.

Scientists group matter into two basic categories: metals and nonmetals. The metals are a huge group of **elements.** Copper, gold, iron, lead, mercury, silver, and tin are examples of metals. Metals often appear shiny because they reflect light well. All metals except mercury are solids at room temperature.

Aluminum is a lightweight metal that can be formed into almost any shape.

Car frames are made from steel, a hard and durable metal.

Metals can be shaped into useful objects. They can be hammered into thin sheets without breaking. They can be drawn into wires.

Most metals are also good **conductors** (carriers of heat and electric current). Have you ever touched a metal spoon sitting in a hot pan? The spoon handle gets hot, even though it's not touching the pan. This is because the metal conducts the heat from one end of the spoon to the other.

Mercury is the only metal that is liquid at room temperature.

Metals are important in building and in making many products. Factories use metals and alloys, or **mixtures** of metals, to make cars and other machines. Metals are also used in making medicines, batteries, and many other products.

Nonmetals

Nonmetals are a much smaller group of **elements** than metals. But nonmetals are more diverse than metals. Carbon, nitrogen, oxygen, and sulfur are a few nonmetals.

Unlike metals, nonmetals are not good **conductors** of heat and electric current. And nonmetals usually appear dull and have a wider range of colors than metals. Solid nonmetals are brittle and break easily. They cannot be shaped.

Nearly all metals are solids at room temperature. But nonmetals can be solids, liquids, or gases.

Helium is a lighter-than-air gas that is used in balloons and parade floats.

Try this!

Nonmetals have many uses. Can you find one example each of the nonmetals hydrogen (H), carbon (C), and oxygen (O) that you use every day? Some examples appear below.

ANSWERS:
Hydrogen: water, hydrogen peroxide (cleaning products, toothpaste)
Carbon: pencil lead
Oxygen: water, air

Neon signs are made of the nonmetallic element neon.

Scientists have also identified a third group of elements—the **metalloids.** Metalloids are chemical elements with some **properties** of metals and some properties of nonmetals. For example, a metalloid may be shiny, but it may not be a good conductor of heat or electricity.

Graphite is a soft steel-gray or black mineral. It is used to make the lead in pencils.

Chlorine kills bacteria (germs) in water. It is widely used to purify drinking water and the water in swimming pools.

The Periodic Table

Where would you go to find information about the different chemical **elements?** Scientists list all of the known chemical elements in a chart called the **periodic table** of elements.

The periodic table lists each element by name or by a one- or two-letter symbol. The symbol "O" stands for oxygen, for example. The symbol for iron is "Fe." The table also lists other important **properties** of the elements.

The periodic table lists each element by name or by a one- or two-letter symbol.

	1								
1	1 **H** Hydrogen	2							
2	3 **Li** Lithium	4 **Be** Beryllium							
3	11 **Na** Sodium	12 **Mg** Magnesium	3	4	5	6	7	8	9
4	19 **K** Potassium	20 **Ca** Calcium	21 **Sc** Scandium	22 **Ti** Titanium	23 **V** Vanadium	24 **Cr** Chromium	25 **Mn** Manganese	26 **Fe** Iron	27 **Co** Cobalt
5	37 **Rb** Rubidium	38 **Sr** Strontium	39 **Y** Yttrium	40 **Zr** Zirconium	41 **Nb** Niobium	42 **Mo** Molybdenum	43 **Tc** Technetium	44 **Ru** Ruthenium	45 **Rh** Rhodium
6	55 **Cs** Cesium	56 **Ba** Barium		72 **Hf** Hafnium	73 **Ta** Tantalum	74 **W** Tungsten	75 **Re** Rhenium	76 **Os** Osmium	77 **Ir** Iridium
7	87 **Fr** Francium	88 **Ra** Radium		104 **Rf** Rutherfordium	105 **Db** Dubnium	106 **Sg** Seaborgium	107 **Bh** Bohrium	108 **Hs** Hassium	109 **Mt** Meitnerium

Metals

Metalloids

Nonmetals

57 **La** Lanthanum	58 **Ce** Cerium	59 **Pr** Praseodymium	60 **Nd** Neodymium	61 **Pm** Promethium	62 **Sm** Samarium	63 **Eu** Europium
89 **Ac** Actinium	90 **Th** Thorium	91 **Pa** Protactinium	92 **U** Uranium	93 **Np** Neptunium	94 **Pu** Plutonium	95 **Am** Americium

Try this!

The chemical elements listed in the periodic table are part of everything in the world. Can you find examples of copper (Cu), iron (Fe), sodium (Na), or aluminum (Al) in objects around the house? What other elements from the periodic table can you find?

The periodic table is arranged by the similarities among elements. For example, metals are listed on the left and center of the table. Nonmetals are on the right. The **metalloids** are found in between.

			13	14	15	16	17	18
								2 **He** Helium
			5 **B** Boron	6 **C** Carbon	7 **N** Nitrogen	8 **O** Oxygen	9 **F** Fluorine	10 **Ne** Neon
10	11	12	13 **Al** Aluminum	14 **Si** Silicon	15 **P** Phosphorus	16 **S** Sulfur	17 **Cl** Chlorine	18 **Ar** Argon
28 **Ni** Nickel	29 **Cu** Copper	30 **Zn** Zinc	31 **Ga** Gallium	32 **Ge** Germanium	33 **As** Arsenic	34 **Se** Selenium	35 **Br** Bromine	36 **Kr** Krypton
46 **Pd** Palladium	47 **Ag** Silver	48 **Cd** Cadmium	49 **In** Indium	50 **Sn** Tin	51 **Sb** Antimony	52 **Te** Tellurium	53 **I** Iodine	54 **Xe** Xenon
78 **Pt** Platinum	79 **Au** Gold	80 **Hg** Mercury	81 **Tl** Thallium	82 **Pb** Lead	83 **Bi** Bismuth	84 **Po** Polonium	85 **At** Astatine	86 **Rn** Radon
110 **Ds** Darmstadtium	111 **Rg** Roentgenium	112 **Cn** Copernicium	113	114	115	116	117	118

64 **Gd** Gadolinium	65 **Tb** Terbium	66 **Dy** Dysprosium	67 **Ho** Holmium	68 **Er** Erbium	69 **Tm** Thulium	70 **Yb** Ytterbium	71 **Lu** Lutetium
96 **Cm** Curium	97 **Bk** Berkelium	98 **Cf** Californium	99 **Es** Einsteinium	100 **Fm** Fermium	101 **Md** Mendelevium	102 **No** Nobelium	103 **Lr** Lawrencium

Glossary

atom one of the tiny particles, or bits, that all matter is made of.

compound matter that is made of two or more different kinds of atoms joined together.

condense to turn a gas into a liquid.

conductor a thing that passes along heat, electricity, light, sound, or another form of energy.

density the amount of matter in a given space.

dimension a measurement of length, breadth, or thickness.

element matter that is made up of only one kind of atom.

evaporate to become a gas.

mass the amount of matter that an object contains.

metalloid an element that has properties of both a metal and a nonmetal.

mixture a combination of two or more different kinds of matter.

molecule a group of joined atoms. A molecule is the smallest piece a compound can be broken into and still stay the same.

periodic table a chart that lists the known chemical elements arranged according to their characteristics.

property a characteristic of matter.

solution a mixture formed by dissolving.

suspension a mixture in which very small particles of a solid remain suspended without dissolving.

volume the amount of space matter takes up in an object.

water vapor water in the form of a gas.

Find Out More

Books

Atoms by Don Nardo (Kidhaven Press, 2002)

Matter: See It, Touch It, Taste It, Smell It by Darlene R. Stille and Sheree Boyd (Picture Window Books, 2004)

Science Measurements: How Heavy? How Long? How Hot? By Chris Eboch and Jon Davis (Picture Window Books, 2007)

Solids, Liquids, and Gases by Darlene R. Stille (Child's World, 2005)

Melting, Freezing, and Boiling: Science Projects With Matter by Robert Gardner (Enslow Elementary, 2006)

Mixtures and Compounds by Alastair Smith, Philip Clarke, and Corinne Henderson (Usborne, 2002)

What Is Mass? by Don L. Curry (Children's Press, 2004)

Websites

All About Atoms
http://education.jlab.org/atomtour/
Dig deeper into the world of matter at this interactive website from the Jefferson Lab (Thomas Jefferson National Accelerator Facility).

The Atom Builder
http://www.pbs.org/wgbh/aso/tryit/atom/
The tiny, mighty atom is made up of even smaller parts! Build your own atoms at this website from PBS's *A Science Odyssey*.

The Atoms Family
http://www.miamisci.org/af/sln/
Learn about the basic building blocks of matter—atoms—at this educational site from the Science Learning Network.

Chem4Kids!
http://www.chem4kids.com/
Basic information about atoms, molecules, elements, and more is available at this educational chemistry site.

Molecularium
http://www.molecularium.com/kidsite.html
At this website, you can travel through the three states of matter with an atomic cast of characters, and build your own molecules in the nanolab.

Strange Matter
http://www.StrangeMatterExhibit.com/
What makes up all the things around us? What makes different materials so different? Find out more about matter and materials at this website.

Study Jams: Solids, Liquids, and Gases
http://teacher.scholastic.com/activities/studyjams/matter_states/
At this site, you can follow along with videos, karaoke, quizzes, and vocabulary exercises to learn about the three states of matter.

Index

Activities